D1242584

Community Helpers
Bus Drivers

by Rebecca Pettiford

Ideas for Parents and Teachers

Bullfrog Books let children practice reading informational text at the earliest reading levels. Repetition, familiar words, and photo labels support early readers.

Before Reading

- Discuss the cover photo. What does it tell them?
- Look at the picture glossary together. Read and discuss the words.

Read the Book

- "Walk" through the book and look at the photos. Let the child ask questions. Point out the photo labels.
- Read the book to the child, or have him or her read independently.

After Reading

- Prompt the child to think more. Ask: Have you ever ridden a bus? Where did the driver take you?

Bullfrog Books are published by Jump!
5357 Penn Avenue South
Minneapolis, MN 55419
www.jumplibrary.com

Copyright © 2015 Jump! International copyright reserved in all countries. No part of this book may be reproduced in any form without written permission from the publisher.

Library of Congress Cataloging-in-Publication Data
Pettiford, Rebecca.
  Bus drivers / by Rebecca Pettiford.
    pages cm. — (Community helpers)
  Includes index.
  Audience: Age 5.
  Audience: Grade K to 3.
  ISBN 978-1-62031-154-7 (hardcover) —
  ISBN 978-1-62496-241-7 (ebook)
  1. Bus drivers — Juvenile literature.
  2. Bus driving — Juvenile literature.
  3. Bus lines — Juvenile literature.
  4. School buses — Juvenile literature. I. Title.
  HD8039.M8P48 2015
  388.3'4233 — dc23
                                         2014032087

Series Editor: Wendy Dieker
Series Designer: Ellen Huber
Book Designer: Anna Peterson
Photo Researcher: Casie Cook

All photos by Shutterstock except: Alamy, 8, 12–13, 14–15, 21, 22, 23br; Getty, cover, 24; iStock, 10–11; SuperStock, 5; Thinkstock, cover, 11, 12, 17, 23tr.

Printed in the United States of America at Corporate Graphics in North Mankato, Minnesota.

Table of Contents

Bus Drivers at Work

Amy wants to
be a bus driver.

What do they do?

They take us where
we need to go.

They keep us safe.

Joe is at the bus yard.

He puts gas in his bus.

He's ready to go!

Fay drives a city bus.
She is on a route.
She has the same
stops each day.

bus route

West 75th Street

Washburn Ave

West 76th Street

Lexington Parkway S

West 79th Street

West 81st Street

Cal drives a shuttle bus.
We are going to the airport.
Cal helps Mr. Lee.

shuttle
bus

13

Len drives a coach bus.
We are going on a trip.
He loads our bags.

coach
bus

15

Mike drives a school bus.

mirror

He sees us in the mirror.

He asks us to sit.

Don's route is over.

He parks at the bus yard.

Bus drivers do good work!

In the Bus

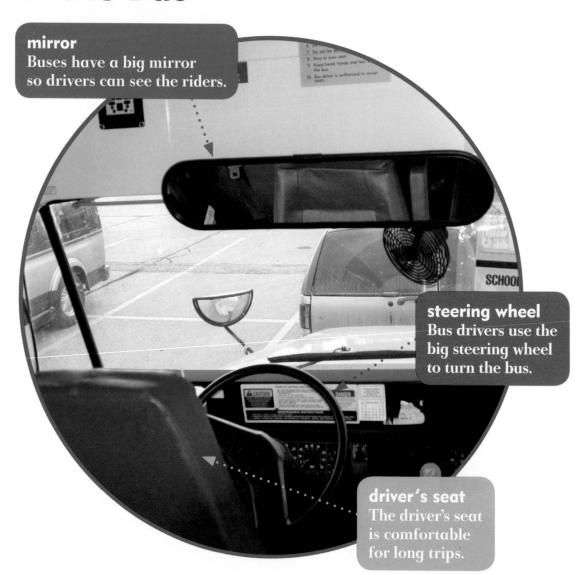

mirror
Buses have a big mirror
so drivers can see the riders.

steering wheel
Bus drivers use the
big steering wheel
to turn the bus.

driver's seat
The driver's seat
is comfortable
for long trips.

Picture Glossary

bus yard
A place where buses are parked.

route
A path a bus takes when picking up and dropping off passengers.

coach bus
A bus that takes riders long distances between two places.

shuttle bus
A bus that takes passengers on short distances between two places.

Index

To Learn More

Learning more is as easy as 1, 2, 3.

1) Go to www.factsurfer.com

2) Enter "bus drivers" into the search box.

3) Click the "Surf" button to see a list of websites.

With factsurfer.com, finding more information is just a click away.

24